I KNOW I CAN

This book belongs to

_____

Date

Dedicated to:
The successful I Know I Can college graduates who walked this path before you.

"Today, we are going to learn about college," said Mrs. Walker.

"College!" said Bonwit Beaver. "What is college?"

"College," said Mrs. Walker, "is a school you go to after you graduate from high school. You go to college to study English, math, science, history, and lots of other subjects, so you can have a good job when you grow up."

"You mean if I go to college, I can become a doctor?"
asked Roxy Rabbit.

"That's right," said Mrs. Walker.

"Roxy, you can't be a doctor," yelled O'Toot, the Owl,
"because you're not as smart as I am."

"O'Toot," said Mrs. Walker, "that is not true.
You all can be whatever you want to be."

"I want to be a builder," said Bonwit Beaver.

"I want to own a store," said Scamper Squirrel.

"You should start planning for college now," said Mrs. Walker.
"You can begin by coming to school every day
and doing all of your work the very best you can."

"Tonight, when you go home," said Mrs. Walker,
"think about a job you would like to have when you grow up."

The bell rang and it was time for the students to go home.

When the students arrived home, they could not stop thinking about college.

"What should I be when I grow up?" asked Bonwit.

"Well, you like to build dams, and you are good at it,"
said Bonwit's mother and father.

"When I grow up, I will go to college to learn how to be a builder.
I KNOW I CAN build houses and tall buildings," said Bonwit.

"What should I be when I grow up?" asked Scamper.

"You are good at gardening and collecting nuts," said Scamper's mother.

"When I grow up," said Scamper, "I will go to college to learn how to run my own grocery store. I KNOW I CAN grow fruits and vegetables, collect nuts, and sell them in my store."

"What should I be when I grow up?" asked Roxy.

"You are good at caring for your brother and sister when they are sick," said Roxy's father.

"When I grow up," said Roxy, "I will go to college to learn to be a doctor.
I KNOW I CAN learn how to make everyone feel better."

"What should I be when I grow up?" asked O'Toot.

"You are good at so many things," said O'Toot's grandmother.

"I am smart and wise. I don't need to decide now what I will do when I grow up. I'm going to watch TV."

The next day, Mrs. Walker said, "Today's assignment is to learn more about the job you would like to have when you grow up. First, you must work on improving the skills that will help you in your job."

"I KNOW I CAN learn how to build a small house," said Bonwit.

"Then, Bonwit, you must practice your math to know how much wood you will need for your house," said Mrs. Walker.

"I KNOW I CAN learn how to sell nuts and food," said Scamper.

"Then, Scamper," said Mrs. Walker, "you will need to read a lot of books to learn how to grow fruits and vegetables. You must also learn how much to charge for the food so that you can make money."

"I KNOW I CAN learn how to help someone who is sick," said Roxy.

"Then, Roxy, you must learn what tools doctors use to make patients feel better," said Mrs. Walker.

"And O'Toot... Where is O'Toot?"

After school that day, Bonwit, Scamper, and Roxy rushed home
to work on their projects, singing as they ran:

"If I try to learn today
About the job I'll have some day,
I KNOW I CAN have lots of fun
Learning how the job is done."

So Bonwit began to build.

Scamper began to collect nuts, gather fruit, and grow vegetables.

Roxy began to help everyone in the neighborhood who didn't feel well.

And O'Toot did nothing!

Each day after school, O'Toot would yell,

"You're wasting your time working on those silly projects.
You could be having fun playing with me.
Do you really think you can go to college?"

"Of course we can go to college," said Bonwit.

"And if you want to go to college," said Roxy, "you should get to work."

Then O'Toot began to notice all of the work that the other students had done during the week.

Bonwit's house was strong.

Scamper had sold a lot of food.

And Roxy had made everyone feel better.

The next day, the students talked about what they had learned.

Except O'Toot!

For once, poor O'Toot had nothing to say.

"If you don't come to class, O'Toot," said Bonwit, "you will not do well in school."
"If you don't work hard," said Scamper, "you won't be able to go to college."
"And, if you don't go to college, it will be hard to get a good job," said Roxy.
O'Toot thought about what the others had said and knew they were right.

"What should I be when I grow up?" asked O'Toot.

"You are good at many things, O'Toot," said Mrs. Walker.
"You can become whatever you want if you try."

"If I begin to work hard now," said O'Toot,
"can I go to college to become a teacher like you, Mrs. Walker?"
"Of course," said Mrs. Walker.

"Then I KNOW I CAN," said O'Toot.

Bonwit, Scamper, and Roxy sang all the way home from school that day, and this time O'Toot joined in!

"Today I'll do my very best.
Until I do, I will not rest.
That's the way I'll get the knowledge.
I KNOW I CAN go on to college."

Activities

Help O'Toot find the way to college.

This is a list of things I like to do.

1. _____
2. _____
3. _____
4. _____
5. _____
6. _____
7. _____
8. _____
9. _____
10. _____

Pages to color

Artist

Nurse

Banker

Scientist

Fire Fighter

Hairdresser

Now it is your turn to draw...

what you want to be.

I should do these things so I can go to college:

1. _____

2. _____

3. _____

4. _____

5. _____

6. _____

7. _____

8. _____

I KNOW I CAN

I KNOW I CAN BE WHAT- EV - ER I CHOOSE

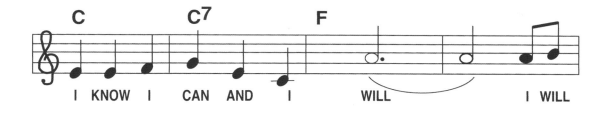

I KNOW I CAN AND I WILL I WILL

WORK EV ERY DAY AND I'LL GET THERE SOME WAY IF I

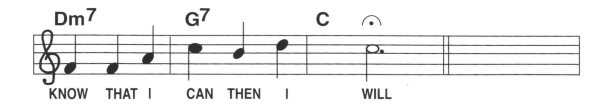

KNOW THAT I CAN THEN I WILL

Make a Commitment to the Future

I will contribute to my community.

I will make a commitment to my parent(s), my teachers, and myself.

I will learn to read.

I will stay in school, work hard, and graduate from high school.

I will plan to go to college.

I BELIEVE IN ME.

_____
Student Signature

_____
Witness (Teacher, Parent, Friend)

_____
Date